Editor
Eric Migliaccio

Managing Editor
Ina Massler Levin, M.A.

Illustrator
Vicki Frazier

Cover Artist
Barb Lorseyedi

Art Production Manager
Kevin Barnes

Imaging
Craig Gunnell
Rosa C. See

Publisher
Mary D. Smith, M.S. Ed.

Author

Maria Elvira Gallardo, M.A.

Teacher Created Resources, Inc.
6421 Industry Way
Westminster, CA 92683
www.teachercreated.com

ISBN: 978-1-4206-3132-6

©2006 Teacher Created Resources, Inc.
Reprinted, 2007
Made in U.S.A.

Table of Contents

Introduction

More than ever, it is important for students to practice writing on a daily basis. Every classroom teacher knows that the key to getting students excited about writing is introducing interesting topics that are fun to write about. *March Daily Journal Writing Prompts* provides kindergarten through second-grade teachers with an entire month of ready-to-use journal topics, including special holiday and seasonal topics for March. All journal topics are included in a calendar that can be easily reproduced for students. A student journal cover allows students to personalize their journal for the month.

Other useful pages that are fun include:

❖ A Blank Calendar (pages 6 and 7)

This can be used to meet your own classroom needs. You may want your students to come up with their own topics for the month, or it may come in handy for homework writing topics.

❖ Word Banks (pages 40–43)

These include commonly-used vocabulary words for school, holiday, and seasonal topics. A blank word bank gives students a place to write other words they have learned throughout the month.

❖ March Author Birthdays (page 44)

Celebrate famous authors' birthdays or introduce an author who is new to your students. This page includes the authors' birthdays and titles of some of their most popular books.

❖ March Historic Events (page 45)

In the format of a time line, this page is a great reference tool for students. They will love seeing amazing events that happened in March.

❖ March Discoveries & Inventions (page 46)

Kindle students' curiosity about discoveries and inventions with this page. This is perfect to use for your science and social-studies classes.

Motivate your students' writing by reproducing the pages in this book and making each student an individual journal. Use all the journal topics included, or pick and choose them as you please. See "Binding Ideas" on page 48 for ways to put it all together. Planning a month of writing will never be easier!

Monthly Calendar

M A R

1	2	3	4
During March, I will probably…	My favorite Dr. Seuss book is…	I consider other people's feelings by…	My favorite thing to talk about is…
9 A fun classroom pet would be…	**10** The telephone was an important invention because…	**11** If I could be a dog, I would be a…	**12** The post office…
17 One day I met a leprechaun, and he….	**18** When I don't behave in class…	**19** When my relatives come to visit…	**20** A great place to go during the weekend is…
25 Right now something I really need is…	**26** If I could create my own holiday, it would be…	**27** A place that seems interesting is…	**28** A big mistake I made once was…

4

Monthly Calendar (cont.)

C H			
5 I'd like to invent a machine that…	**6** The person who knows me the best is…	**7** If we had a new student in our class, I would…	**8** An important woman in history is…
13 I really want to save money for…	**14** The toys I'll never give up are…	**15** The best things about my neighborhood are…	**16** If I were a superhero, I'd save people from…
21 Newspapers help people know…	**22** If I had to move and could only take three things…	**23** My idea of a perfect day is…	**24** A movie about my life would…
29 Books will always be special in my life because…	**30** Doctors are important because they…	**31** I like going to the market…	**Special Topic** **Spring** Now that spring is here…

Blank Monthly Calendar

M A R

1	2	3	4
9	10	11	12
17	18	19	20
25	26	27	28

Blank Monthly Calendar (cont.)

C H			
5	6	7	8
13	14	15	16
21	22	23	24
29	30	31	Free Choice Topic

During March, I will probably _____

_____

_____

_____

_____

_____

_____

                                      _____

                                      _____

                                      _____

My favorite Dr. Seuss book is _____

_____

_____

_____

_____

_____

_____

_____

_____

I consider other people's feelings by _____

_____

_____

_____

_____

_____

_____

_____

My favorite thing to talk about is _____

_____

_____

_____

_____

_____

_____

_____

"And then I..."

I'd like to invent a machine that _____

_____

_____

_____

_____

_____

_____

_____

_____

_____

The person who knows me the best is

_____

_____

_____

_____

_____

_____

If we had a new student in our class, I would

_____

_____

_____

_____

_____

_____

An important woman in history is _____

_____

_____

_____

_____

_____

_____

_____

A fun classroom pet would be _____

_____

_____

_____

_____

_____

_____

The telephone was an important invention
because _____

_____

_____

_____

_____

_____

_____

_____

_____

If I could be a dog, I would be a _____

_____

_____

_____

_____

_____

_____

_____

_____

The post office _____

_____

_____

_____

_____

_____

_____

_____

I really want to save money for _____

_____

_____

_____

_____

_____

_____

_____

The toys I'll never give up are _____

_____

_____

_____

_____

_____

_____

_____

The best things about my neighborhood are

_____

_____

_____

_____

_____

_____

_____

_____

If I were a superhero, I'd save people from

_____

_____

_____

_____

_____

_____

_____

_____

One day, I met a leprechaun, and he

_____

_____

_____

_____

_____

_____

_____

_____

When I don't behave in class _____

_____

_____

_____

_____

_____

_____

_____

_____

When my relatives come to visit _____

_____

_____

_____

_____

_____

_____

_____

_____

_____

A great place to go during the weekend is

_____

_____

_____

_____

_____

_____

Now Playing
The Great
Horse Race

Theatre

_____

Newspapers help people know _____

_____

_____

_____

_____

_____

_____

_____

                              _____

                              _____

                              _____

If I had to move and could only take three things _____

_____

_____

_____

_____

_____

_____

_____

_____

My idea of a perfect day is _____

_____

_____

_____

_____

_____

_____

_____

_____

A movie about my life would_____

_____

_____

_____

_____

_____

_____

_____

_____

_____

Right now something I really need is

_____

_____

_____

_____

_____

_____

_____

_____

_____

If I could create my own holiday, it would be

_____

_____

_____

_____

_____

Best Friends Day!

A place that seems interesting is _____

_____

_____

_____

_____

_____

_____

_____

_____

A big mistake I made once was _____

_____

_____

_____

_____

_____

_____

_____

_____

Books will always be special in my life because _____

_____

_____

_____

_____

_____

_____

_____

_____

_____

_____

Doctors are important because they

_____

_____

_____

_____

_____

_____

_____

_____

I like going to the market _____

_____

_____

_____

_____

_____

Now that spring is here _____

_____

_____

_____

_____

_____

_____

_____

_____

School Word Bank

alphabet	desks	map	recess
art	dictionary	markers	report card
assembly	encyclopedia	math	rules
award	folder	notebook	science
binder	glue	office	scissors
board	grades	paper	stapler
books	history	pencils	study
bus	homework	pens	subject
children	journal	playground	teacher
class	learning	principal	thesaurus
crayons	lunch	reading	write

Holiday Word Bank

March Holidays

Doctor's Day	Women's History Month
St. Patrick's Day	World Reading Month

accomplishments	important	patients
author	intelligent	pediatrician
books	Ireland	pot
bookstore	Irish	publisher
caring	legend	rainbow
doctor	leprechaun	read
equal rights	library	school
famous	luck	shamrock
gold	magazine	special
green	magic	story
healthcare	medicine	suffrage
history	newspaper	wish
hospital	office	women
illustrator	operation	world

Seasonal Word Bank

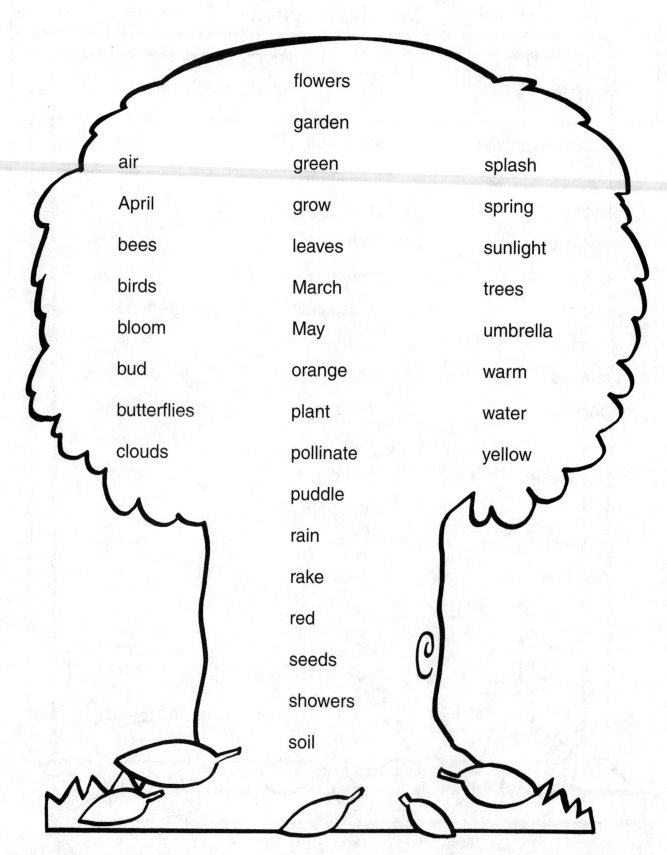

flowers

garden

air green splash

April grow spring

bees leaves sunlight

birds March trees

bloom May umbrella

bud orange warm

butterflies plant water

clouds pollinate yellow

puddle

rain

rake

red

seeds

showers

soil

My Word Bank

March Author Birthdays

2

Dr. Seuss
(1904–1991)

The Cat in the Hat
(Random House, 1957)
Green Eggs and Ham
(Random House, 1960)

3

Patricia
MacLachlan
(b. 1938)

Through Grandpa's
Eyes
(HarperCollins, 1980)
Who Loves Me?
(Joanna Cotler, 2005)

6

Thacher Hurd
(b. 1949)

Mama Don't Allow
(HarperCollins, 1984)
Art Dog
(HarperCollins, 1996)

10

Jack Kent
(b. 1920)

The Caterpillar and
the Polliwog
(Simon &
Schuster, 1982)
Round Robin
(Prentice Hall, 1984)

11

Ezra Jack Keats
(1916–1983)

The Snowy Day
(Viking Books, 1962)
Peter's Chair
Puffin Books, 1998

13

Diane Dillon
(b. 1933)

To Every Thing There
Is a Season
(Blue Sky Press, 1998)
Rap a Tap Tap
(Blue Sky Press, 2002)

17

Penelope Lively
(b. 1933)

Boy Without a Name
(Houghton Mifflin)
Good Night,
Sleep Tight
(Candlewick
Press, 1995)

20

Mitsumasa Anno
(b. 1926)

Anno's Magic Seeds
(Philomel Books)
Anno's Journey
Putnam, 1997)

20

Ellen Conford
(b. 1942)

Me and the
Terrible Two
(Little Brown
& Co., 1974)
Eugene the Brave
(Little Brown
& Co., 1978)

26

Betty MacDonald
(1908–1958)

Mrs. Piggle-Wiggle
(Harper Trophy,1985)
The Egg and I
(Perennial, 1987)

28

Mary Stolz
(b. 1920)

Storm in the Night
(HarperCollins, 1988)
Emmett's Pig
(HarperCollins, 2003)

28

Byrd Baylor
(b. 1924)

Amigo
(Aladdin, 1989)
The Table Where
Rich People Sit
(Atheneum, 1994)

March Historic Events

March 1, 1872
Yellowstone National Park was established as the world's first national park.

March 3, 1931
The bill designating "The Star-Spangled Banner" as our national anthem was adopted by the U.S. Senate.

March 4, 1789
The first U.S. Congress met in New York City and declared that the new Constitution of the U.S. was in effect.

March 6, 1836
"Alamo Day" commemorates the day when 187 Texans died fighting for independence from Mexico.

March 10, 1876
The first telephone message was transmitted on this day by Alexander Graham Bell.

March 11, 1702
The first regular English-language newspaper, the "Daily Courant," was published for the first time.

March 12, 1789
The United States Post Office was established.

March 17, 1756
St. Patrick's Day was celebrated in New York City for the first time.

March 22, 1972
The Equal Rights Amendment, which prohibited discrimination based on gender, was passed and submitted by the Senate for ratification by the states.

March Discoveries & Inventions

3   **Guam was discovered** in 1521 by Magellan.

4   **The microphone was invented** by Emile Berliner in 1877.

7   **The patent for the telephone was granted** to Alexander Graham Bell in 1876.

     The discovery of the South Pole was announced by Roald Amundsen in 1912.

13   **The planet Uranus was discovered** in 1781 by German-born English astronomer Sir William Herschel.

     Earmuffs were patented by Chester Greenwood of Maine in 1887.

14   **The patent for the cotton gin was granted** to Eli Whitney in 1794.

17   **The first rubber band was patented** by Stephen Perry of London in 1845.

22   **The first patent for a laser** (light amplification by stimulated emission of radiation) was granted to Arthur Schawlow and Charles Townes in 1960.

25   **Saturn's largest moon, Titan, was discovered** in 1655 by Christian Huygens.

27   **Explorer Ponce de León sighted North America** (specifically, Florida) in 1513 for the first time. He mistook it for another island.

30   **Anesthetic was first used in surgery** in 1842. Dr. Crawford W. Long removed a tumor from the neck of a man under the influence of ether.

     The first pencil with an eraser top was patented by Hyman Lipman in 1858.

March Journal

by

_____

Binding Ideas

Students will be so delighted when they see a month of their writing come together with one of the following binding ideas. You may choose to bind their journals at the beginning or end of the month, once they have already filled all of the journal topic pages. When ready to bind students' journals, have them color in their journal cover on page 47. It may be a good idea to reproduce the journal covers on hard stock paper in order to better protect the pages in the journal. Use the same hard stock paper for the back cover.

Simple Book Binding

1. Put all pages in order and staple together along the left margin.

2. Cut book-binding tape to the exact length of the book.

3. Run the center line of tape along the left side of the book and fold to cover the front left margin and the back right margin. Your book is complete!

Yarn-Sewn Binding

1. Put all pages in order and hole-punch the left margin.

2. Stitch the pages together with thick yarn or ribbon.

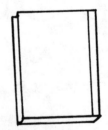